CONGAREE NATIONAL PARK ACTIVITY BOOK

PUZZLES, MAZES, GAMES, AND MORE ABOUT CONGAREE NATIONAL PARK

NATIONAL PARKS ACTIVITIES SERIES

CONGAREE NATIONAL PARK ACTIVITY BOOK

Copyright 2022
Published by Little Bison Press

The author acknowledges that the lands on which
Congaree National Park is located are the traditional lands of
Tsalaguwetiyi (Cherokee, East) and Congaree Tribes.

LITTLE BISON
Press

For more free national parks activities, visit
www.littlebisonpress.com

About Congaree National Park

Congaree National Park is located in South Carolina less than 20 miles from the state's capital, Columbia. Before it became designated as a national park in 2003, it was known as Congaree Swamp National Monument. This name was misleading, because it wasn't a swamp at all! The floodplain does not have water covering it all year-round, which means it is not a swamp.

This park is famous for having over 25 miles of hiking trails, including 2.4 miles of boardwalk that allows visitors to explore the floodplains of the Congaree river. Cedar Creek offers canoeing and kayaking trails through a primeval old-growth forest containing some of the tallest trees in eastern North America.

Visitors can visit Congaree Bluffs Heritage Preserve on the park's south side. The Preserve offers many hiking paths that cover just over two hundred acres of hickory, oak, and tupelo forest.

Congaree National Park is famous for:
- 25 miles of hiking trails
- canoeing and kayaking trails
- primeval old-growth forests

Hey, I'm Parker!

I'm the only snail in history to visit every National Park in the United States! Come join me on my adventures in Congaree National Park.

Throughout this book, we will learn about the history of the park, the animals and plants that live here, and things to do if you ever visit in person. This book is also full of games and activities!

Last but not least, I am hidden 9 times on different pages. See how many times you can find me. This page doesn't count!

Congaree Bingo

Let's play bingo! Cross off each box you are able to during your visit to the national park. Try to get a bingo down, across, or diagonally. If you can't visit the park, use the bingo board to plan your perfect trip.

Pick out some activities you would want to do during your visit. What would you do first? How long would you spend there? What animals would you try to see?

SPOT A SALAMANDER	SEE AN ALLIGATOR	GO FOR A HIKE	TAKE A PICTURE AT AN OVERLOOK	IDENTIFY A TREE
VISIT THE BOOKSTORE AT THE VISITORS CENTER	LEARN ABOUT THE INDIGENOUS PEOPLE WHO LIVE IN THIS AREA	WITNESS A SUNRISE OR SUNSET	OBSERVE THE NIGHT SKIES	GO FISHING
HEAR A BIRD CALL	SPOT A WINDING RIVER	FREE SPACE	LEARN ABOUT THE IMPORTANCE OF FIRE TO CONGAREE'S ECOSYSTEM	SPOT SOME ANIMAL TRACKS
PICK UP TEN PIECES OF TRASH	HAVE A PICNIC	SEE A WHITE-TAILED DEER	WALK ON THE BOARDWALK TRAIL	SPOT A BIRD OF PREY
LEARN ABOUT THE CHAMPION TREES	SEE SOMEONE IN A CANOE	GO CAMPING	VISIT A RANGER STATION	PARTICIPATE IN A RANGER-LED ACTIVITY

Bird Scavenger Hunt

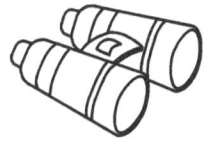

Congaree National Park is a great place to go birdwatching. You don't have to be able to identify different species of birds in order to have fun. Open your eyes and tune in your ears. Check off as many birds on this list as you can.

☐ A colorful bird   ☐ A big bird

☐ A brown bird   ☐ A small bird

☐ A bird in a tree   ☐ A hopping bird

☐ A bird with long tail feathers   ☐ A flying bird

☐ A bird making noise   ☐ A bird's nest

☐ A bird eating or hunting   ☐ A bird's footprint on the ground

☐ A bird with spots   ☐ A bird with stripes

What was the easiest bird on the list to find? What was the hardest?
Why do you think that was?

_____

_____

_____

Take a Hike

Go for a hike with your friends or family. If you aren't able to visit Congaree National Park, go for a walk in a park near where you live. Read through the prompts before your walk and finish the activities after you return.

Draw something you saw that moves:

Draw something you saw when you looked up:

Draw something you saw in the water:

Draw a picture of your favorite part of the walk:

Design a Sweatshirt

Imagine you are a graphic designer and you have been hired to design a sweatshirt that will be for sale in the Harry Hampton Visitor Center. Use your knowledge of Congaree National Park to create a meaningful souvenir.

Your design should include:

- the name of the park
- the year the park was established
- 2 or more colors that represent the park
- 1 symbol or feature of the park

Use colored pencils, crayons, or markers to make your designs. You can include artwork on the sleeves too!

Go Canoeing on the Congaree River Blue Trail

DID YOU KNOW?

The Congaree River Blue Trail is a 50-mile designated recreational paddling trail, extending from the state capital of Columbia, downstream to Congaree National Park.

start here →

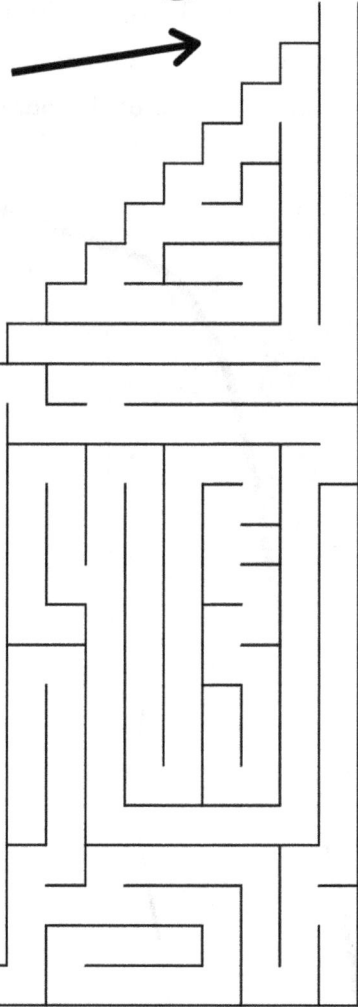

Camping Packing List

What should you take with you when you go camping? Pretend you are in charge of your family camping trip. Make a list of what you would need to be safe and comfortable on an overnight excursion. Some considerations are listed on the side.

1.
2.
3.
4.
5.
6.
7.
8.
9.
10.
11.
12.
13.
14.
15.
16.

- What will you eat at every meal?

- What will the weather be like?

- Where will you sleep?

- What will you do during your free time?

- How luxurious do you want your camp to be?

- How will you cook?

- How will you see at night?

- How will you dispose of trash?

- What might you need in case of emergencies?

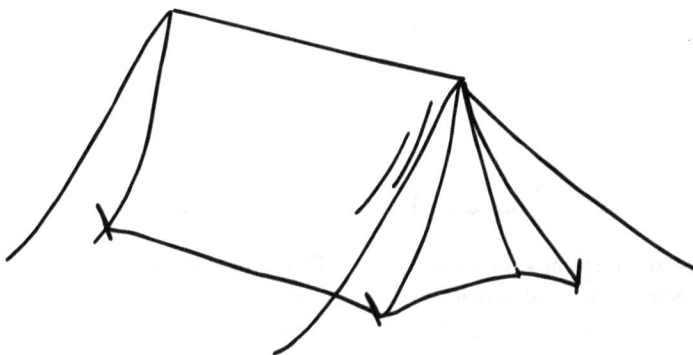

Congaree National Park

Date: _____   Season: _____

Who I went with: _____   Weather: _____

How was your experience? Write a few sentences about your trip. Where did you stay? What did you do? What was your favorite activity? If you haven't visited the park yet, write a paragraph pretending that you did.

_____

_____

_____

_____

_____

STAMPS

Many national parks and monuments have cancellation stamps for visitors to use. These rubber stamps record the date and location that you visited. Many people collect the markings as a free souvenir. Check with a ranger to see where you can find a stamp during your visit. If you aren't able to find one, you can draw your own.

Where is the Park?

Congaree National Park is in the southeastern United States. It is located in South Carolina, nicknamed the Palmetto State. While you may see many other palmetto trees in South Carolina, the foremost trees you will see at Congaree are loblolly pines and bald cypresses.

South Carolina

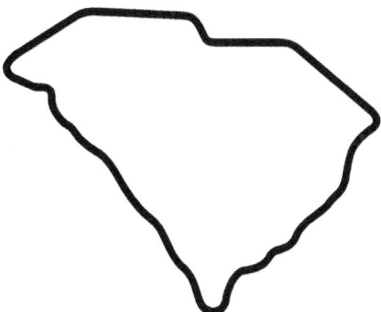

Look at the shape of South Carolina. Can you find it on the map? If you are from the US, can you find your home state? Color South Carolina blue. Put a star on the map where you live.

Connect the Dots #1

Connect the dots to figure out what this tiny critter is. The Ruby-Throated species of this animal lives in Congaree National Park.

Their heart rate can reach as high as 1,260 beats per minute and a breathing rate of 250 breaths per minute. Have you ever measured your breathing rate? Ask a friend or family member to set a timer for 60 seconds. Once they say "go," try to breathe normally. Count each breath until they say "stop." How do your breaths per minute compare to hummingbirds?

_____

_____

Being Respectful

Rangers need your help! Some people toss their trash where they shouldn't, create graffiti, or take artifacts when they visit Congaree National Park. In the space below, create a poster to help show other visitors how to be respectful.

Who Lives Here?

Below are 8 plants and animals that live in the park.
Use the word bank to fill in the clues below.

WORD BANK: BEAVER, OSPREY, ALLIGATOR, COYOTE, BUCKEYE, COTTONMOUTH, BOBCAT, VELVET ANT

☐ ☐ C ☐ ☐ ☐

☐ O ☐ ☐ ☐

☐ ☐ ☐ ☐ N ☐ ☐ ☐ ☐

☐ ☐ ☐ G ☐ ☐ ☐

☐ ☐ ☐ A ☐

☐ ☐ ☐ R ☐ ☐

☐ ☐ ☐ ☐ E ☐ ■ ☐ ☐ ☐

☐ E ☐ ☐ ☐

Animals of Congaree National Park

Beavers
are the largest North American rodent.

Shrews may have toxic saliva they use to subdue their prey.

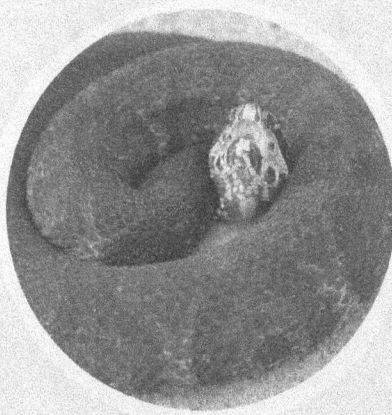

Cottonmouths
are a common sight along the parks, waterways and trails.

Ospreys mostly eat fish but may sometimes eat lizards, muskrats, or even squirrels.

Opossums,
or known simply as possums, are the only marsupial native to the United States.

Common Names
vs.
Scientific Names

A common name of an organism is a name that is based on everyday language. You have heard the common names of plants, animals, and other living things on tv, in books, and at school. Common names can also be referred to as "English" names, popular names, or farmer's names. Common names can vary from place to place. The word for a particular tree may be one thing, but that same tree has a different name in another country. Common names can even vary from region to region, even in the same country.

Scientific names, or Latin names, are given to organisms to make it possible to have uniform names for the same species. Scientific names are in Latin. You may have heard plants or animals referred to by their scientific name or parts of their scientific names. Latin names are also called "binomial nomenclature," which refers to a two-part naming system. The first part of the name - the generic name - refers to the genus to which the species belongs. The second part of the name, the specific name, identifies the species. For example, Tyrannosaurus rex is an example of a widely known scientific name.

Coyote

Canis latrans

COMMON NAME

North American Beaver

Castor canadensis

LATIN NAME = GENUS + SPECIES

Coyote = Canis latrans

North American Beaver = Castor canadensis

Find the Match!
Common Names and Latin Names

Match the common name to the scientific name for each animal. The first one is done for you. Use clues on the page before and after this one to complete the matches.

Gray Fox — Haliaeetus leucocephalus

Loblolly Pine — Lontra canadensis

Bald Cypress — Butorides virescens

River Otter — Sylvilagus palustris

Great Horned Owl — Pinus taeda

Bald Eagle — Agkistrodon contortrix

Green Heron — Bubo virginianus

Marsh Rabbit — Urocyon cinereoargenteus

Copperhead — Taxodium distichum

Bald Eagle

Haliaeetus leucocephalus

Green Heron
Butorides Birescens

River Otter
Lontra canadensis

Great Horned Owl
Bubo virginianus

**Some plants
and animals
that live at
Congaree NP**

Loblolly Pine
Pinus taeda

Marsh Rabbit
Sylvilagus palustris

Copperhead
Agkistrondon contortrix

Things To Do Jumble

Unscramble the letters to uncover activities you can do while in Congaree National Park. Hint: each one ends in -ing.

1. YAKKA
   ☐☐☐☐☐☐ ING

2. IHK
   ☐☐☐ ING

3. DBIR
   ☐☐☐☐ ING

4. MACP
   ☐☐☐☐ ING

5. KINICPC
   ☐☐☐☐☐☐☐ ING

6. EISSTEHG
   ☐☐☐☐☐☐☐☐ ING

7. SARTGZA
   ☐☐☐☐☐☐☐ ING

Word Bank

birding
reading
camping
stargazing
kayaking
hiking
hunting
singing
boating
sightseeing
picnicking

Making a Difference

It is important to protect the valuable resources of the world, not only beautiful places like national parks.

How many of these things do you do at home? If you answered "no" to more than 10 items, talk to the grownups in your life to see if there are any household habits you might be able to change. Conserving our collective resources helps us all.

Yes	No	Do you...
☐	☐	turn off the water when brushing your teeth?
☐	☐	use LED light bulbs when possible?
☐	☐	use a reusable water bottle instead of disposable ones?
☐	☐	ride your bike or take the bus instead of riding in the car?
☐	☐	have a rain barrel under your roof gutters to collect rain water?
☐	☐	take quick showers?
☐	☐	avoid putting more food on your plate than you will eat?
☐	☐	take reusable lunch containers?
☐	☐	grow a garden?
☐	☐	buy items with less packaging?
☐	☐	recycle paper?
☐	☐	recycle plastic?
☐	☐	have a compost pile at home so you can make your own soil?
☐	☐	pick up trash when you see it on the trail?
☐	☐	plan a "staycation" and fly only when you have to?

_____ _____
of   # of
Yes   No

Add up your score! Are there any "no"s that you want to turn into a yes?

Can you think of any other ways to protect our natural resources?

_____

Map Symbol Sudoku

The National Park System creates park maps using symbols instead of words. They are easily understood and take up much less space on a tiny map.

Trailhead	Cabin	Wildlife	Campground

Complete this symbol sudoku puzzle. Fill each square with one of the symbols. Each one can appear only once in each row, column, and mini 2x2 grid. Each symbol means something, so you can write what the symbol represents instead of drawing the symbols if you prefer.

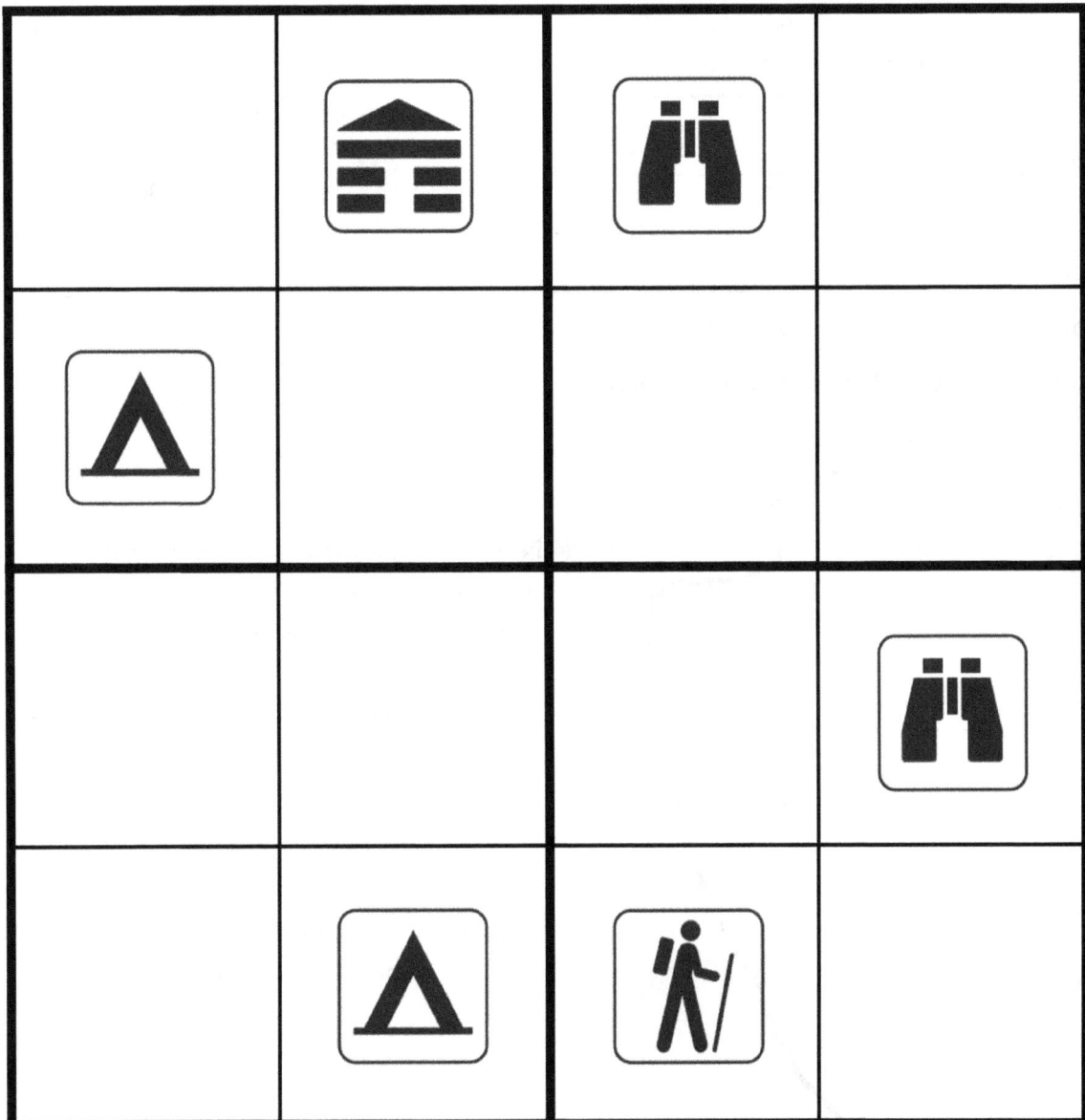

	Cabin	Wildlife	
Campground			
			Wildlife
	Campground	Trailhead	

The National Park Logo

The National Park System has over 400 units in the US. Just like Congaree National Park, each location is unique or special in some way. The areas include other national parks, historic sites, monuments, seashores, and other recreation areas.

Each element of the National Park emblem represents something that the National Park Service protects. Fill in each blank below to show what each symbol represents.

```
WORD BANK:
_____
MOUNTAINS, ARROWHEAD, BISON,
SEQUOIA TREE, WATER
```

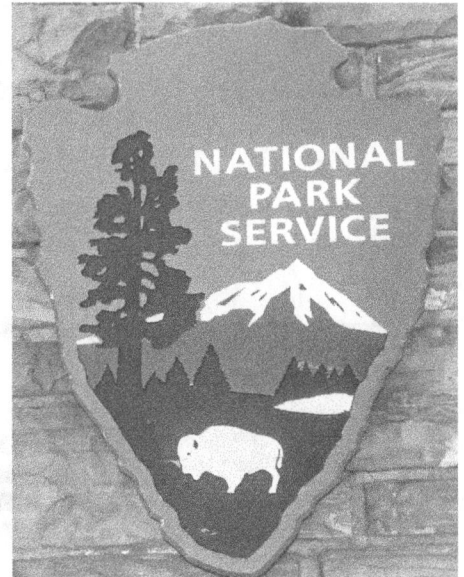

This represents all plants: _____

This represents all animals: _____

This represents the landscapes: _____

This represents the waters protected by the park service: _____

This represents the historical and archeological values: _____

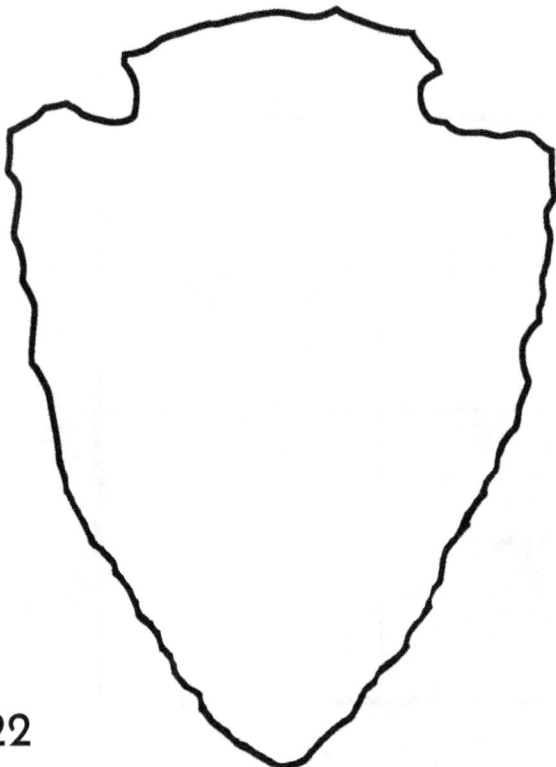

Now it's your turn! Pretend you are designing a new national park. Add elements to the design that represent the things your park protects.

What is the name of your park?

Describe why you included the symbols that you chose. What do they mean?

The Ten Essentials

Careful preparation and knowledge are key to a successful adventure into Congaree's backcountry.

The ten essentials are a list of things that are important to have when you go for longer hikes. If you go on a hike to the <u>backcountry,</u> it is especially important that you have everything you need in case of an emergency. If you get lost or something unforeseen happens, it is good to be prepared to survive until help finds you.

The ten essentials list was developed in the 1930s by an outdoors group called the Mountaineers. Over time and technological advancements, this list has evolved. Can you identify all the things on the current list? Circle each of the "essentials" and cross out everything that doesn't make the cut.

fire: matches, lighter, tinder, and/or stove	a pint of milk	extra money	headlamp, plus extra batteries	extra clothes
extra water	a dog	Polaroid camera	bug net	lightweight games, like a deck of cards
extra food	a roll of duct tape	shelter	sun protection, such as sunglasses, sun-protective clothes, and sunscreen	knife, plus a gear repair kit
a mirror	navigation: map, compass, altimeter, GPS device, or satellite messenger	first aid kit	extra flip-flops	entertainment, such as video games or books

Backcountry - a remote, undeveloped rural area.

Connect the Dots #2

This animal lives in almost every state in the US, including Congaree National Park. They are nocturnal, more active at night, and sleep during the day. They are omnivorous eaters, meaning they eat both plants and animals.

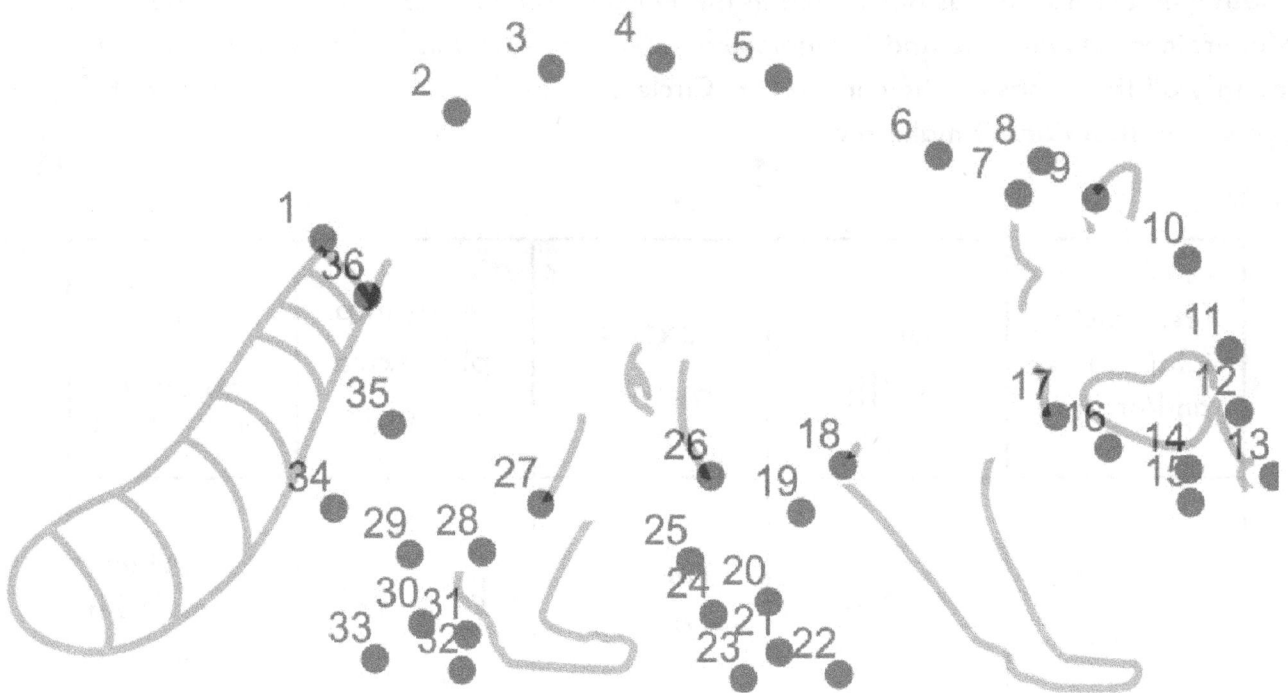

Are you an omnivore like a raccoon? An herbivore only eats plant foods. A carnivore only eats meat. An omnivore eats both. What type of eater are you? Write down some of your favorite foods to back up your answer.

_____

_____

Congaree Word Search

Words may be horizontal, vertical, diagonal,
or they might even be backwards!

1. mosquitos
2. boardwalk
3. cypresses
4. turtles
5. woodpeckers
6. snakes
7. swamp
8. south
9. carolina
10. floodplain
11. bottomland
12. oxbow
13. fireflies
14. knees
15. eastover
16. southeast
17. sierra club

```
O X B O W T H W E S T L O W C
A B O A R D W A L K E L A N A
N G K S O T I U Q S O M A F N
I M P N Y T H T W O R G D L O
L I A D E A L L O E I S I O E
O O N D D E A A C T W K O I
R E S E E H S O U T H A I D N
A L B A N U I E G E N M N P G
C Y P R E S S E S B C P G L E
P C T S A E H T U O S I O A A
T U R T L E S L O I K E T I N
S R N I K O C I O V O K I N E
N I O F E A S T O V E R L G W
A C G F R O V E P O O R V E H
K I L R K D N A L M O T T O B
E T E I A E E G E Z E P R N L
S I W O O D P E C K E R S I E
S E I L F E R I F Y M A L A Z
```

25

Wildlife Wisdom

The national park is home to many different kinds of animals. Seeing wildlife can be an exciting part of visiting the national park but it is important to remember that these animals are wild. They need plenty of space and a healthy habitat where they can find their own food. Part of this is not allowing animals to eat any human food. This is their home and we are the visitors. We need to be respectful of the wildlife in the park.

Directions: Circle the highlighted words that best complete the following sentences.

If an animal changes its behavior because of your presence, you are:
    A) too close
    B) funny looking
    C) dehydrated and should drink more water

The best thing we can do to help wild animals survive is:
    A) make them pets
    B) protect their habitat
    C) knit them winter sweaters

In a national park, it is okay to share your food with wild animals:
    A) never
    B) always
    C) sometimes

When you're hiking in an area where there are bears, you should warn bears that you are entering their space by:
    A) hiking quietly
    B) making noise
    C) wearing bright colors

At night, park rangers care for the animals by:
    A) putting them back into their cages
    B) tucking them into bed
    C) leaving them alone

If you see an abandoned bird's nest, it is best to:
    A) pet the baby birds
    B) leave it alone
    C) crunch the empty eggshells

Bears look under logs in hopes of finding:
    A) granola bars
    B) insects
    C) peanuts to eat

The place where an animal lives is called its:
    A) condo
    B) habitat
    C) crib

The Perfect Picnic Spot

Fill in the blanks on this page without looking at the full story. Once you have each line filled out, use the words you've chosen to complete the story on the next page.

EMOTION _____

FOOD _____

SOMETHING SWEET _____

STORE _____

MODE OF TRANSPORTATION _____

NOUN _____

SOMETHING ALIVE _____

SAUCE _____

PLURAL VEGETABLES _____

ADJECTIVE _____

PLURAL BODY PART _____

ANIMAL _____

PLURAL FRUIT _____

PLACE _____

SOMETHING TALL _____

COLOR _____

ADJECTIVE _____

NOUN _____

A DIFFERENT ANIMAL _____

FAMILY MEMBER #1 _____

FAMILY MEMBER #2 _____

VERB THAT ENDS IN -ING _____

A DIFFERENT FOOD _____

The Perfect Picnic Spot

Use the words from the previous page to complete a silly story.

When my family suggested having our lunch at the Congaree Picnic Shelter, I

was _____. I love eating my _____ outside! I knew we had picked up a
     EMOTION   FOOD

box of _____ from the _____ for after lunch, my favorite. We drove up
    SOMETHING SWEET   STORE

to the area and I jumped out of the _____. "I will find the perfect spot for
                                    MODE OF TRANSPORTATION

a picnic!" I grabbed a _____ for us to sit on, and I ran off. I passed a picnic
                      NOUN

table, but it was covered with _____ so we couldn't sit there. The next
                              SOMETHING ALIVE

picnic table looked okay, but there were smears of _____ and pieces of
                                                  SAUCE

_____ everywhere. The people that were there before must have been
PLURAL VEGETABLES

_____! I gritted my _____ together and kept walking down the path,
ADJECTIVE   PLURAL BODY PART

determined to find the perfect spot. I wanted a table with a good view of the

trees. Why was this so hard? If we were lucky, I might even get to see _____
                                                                      ANIMAL

eating some _____ on the rocks. They don't have those in _____, where I
           PLURAL FRUIT   PLACE

am from. I walked down a little hill and there it was, the perfect spot! The trees

towered overhead and looked as tall as _____. The patch of grass was a
                                       SOMETHING TALL

beautiful _____ color. The _____ flowers were growing on
         COLOR   ADJECTIVE

the side of a _____. I looked across the forests edge and even saw a
             NOUN

_____ on the edge of a rock. I looked back to see my _____ and
DIFFERENT ANIMAL   FAMILY MEMBER #1

_____ _____ a picnic basket. "I hope you brought plenty of
FAMILY MEMBER #2 VERB THAT ENDS IN ING

_____, I'm starving!"
A DIFFERENT FOOD   29

Hike the Boardwalk Loop Trail

start here →

Congaree Waterways
Word Search

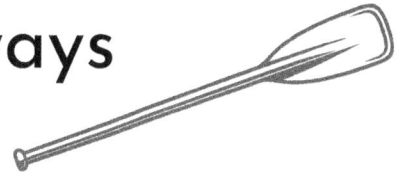

Congaree National Park is a floodplain forest. Waters from the Congaree and Wateree Rivers sweep through the floodplain, carrying nutrients and sediments that nourish and rejuvenate this ecosystem.

1. canoe
2. kayak
3. paddle
4. alligator
5. Cedar Creek
6. old-growth
7. safety
8. hazard
9. log jam
10. caution
11. aquatic
12. habitat
13. turtle
14. snag
15. explore
16. water

```
H A B I T A T R E S K L O W K
H T A S K I L E R O L P X E J
T E P R C A N O E C L B A P B
S M P A G P T U R T L E U H C
C E C E D A R C R E E K J A L
A O L D G C O A E C T E A Z I
R E S I E H E K L N K A Y A K
P L L A M U I E D W N E K R G
R L H S G M L O D E I D Y D M
A C C I T A U Q A I P H O E A
L O G J A M I N P O K T N S N
S R N I K O S I S M O W I R P
W I O S N I A L P D O O L F W
A C G O L O F E S O O R V E H
T I C C A U T I O N A G A N S
E T T F A E E G L Z E D Q N L
R Y D R O E Y E C T R L C E E
C J D O S N E D N Y M O L A M
```

Leave No Trace Quiz

Leave No Trace is a concept that helps people make decisions during outdoor recreation that protects the environment. There are seven principles that guide us when we spend time outdoors, whether you are in a national park or not. Are you an expert in Leave No Trace? Take this quiz and find out!

1. How can you plan ahead and prepare to ensure you have the best experience you can in the national park?
    a. Make sure you stop by the ranger station for a map and to ask about current conditions.
    b. Just wing it! You will know the best trail when you see it.
    c. Stick to your plan, even if conditions change. You traveled a long way to get here, and you should stick to your plan.
2. What is an example of traveling on a durable surface?
    a. Walking only on the designated path.
    b. Walking on the grass that borders the trail if the trail is very muddy.
    c. Taking a shortcut if you can find one because it means you will be walking less.
3. Why should you dispose of waste properly?
    a. You don't need to. Park rangers love to pick up the trash you leave behind.
    b. You should actually leave your leftovers behind, because animals will eat them. It is important to make sure they aren't hungry.
    c. So that other peoples' experiences of the park are not impacted by you leaving your waste behind.
4. How can you best follow the concept "leave what you find?"
    a. Take only a small rock or leaf to remember your trip.
    b. Take pictures, but leave any physical items where they are.
    c. Leave everything you find, unless it may be rare like an arrowhead, then it is okay to take.
5. What is not a good example of minimizing campfire impacts?
    a. Only having a campfire in a pre-existing campfire ring.
    b. Checking in with current conditions when you consider making a campfire.
    c. Building a new campfire ring in a location that has a better view.
6. What is a poor example of respecting wildlife?
    a. Building squirrel houses out of rocks so the squirrels have a place to live.
    b. Stay far away from wildlife and give them plenty of space.
    c. Reminding your grown-ups not to drive too fast in animal habitats while visiting the park.
7. How can you show consideration of other visitors?
    a. Play music on your speaker so other people at the campground can enjoy it.
    b. Wear headphones on the trail if you choose to listen to music.
    c. Make sure to yell "Hello!" to every animal you see at top volume.

Park Poetry

America's parks inspire art of all kinds. Painters, sculptors, photographers, writers, and artists of all mediums have taken inspiration from natural beauty. They have turned their inspiration into great works.

Use this space to write your own poem about the park. Think about what you have experienced or seen. Use descriptive language to create an acrostic poem. This type of poem has the first letter of each line spell out another word. Create an acrostic that spells out the word "Forest."

F _____

O _____

R _____

E _____

S _____

T _____

Full of life

Open skies

Ready for adventure

Exploring new places

So many

Tall trees

Fresh air

Outdoors

Really hot

Everyone is

Sweating

Time to go fishing!

Take in the Teeny-Tiny

Take a walk through the floodplain and draw examples of teensy things you can find such as little plants, bugs, and pebbles.

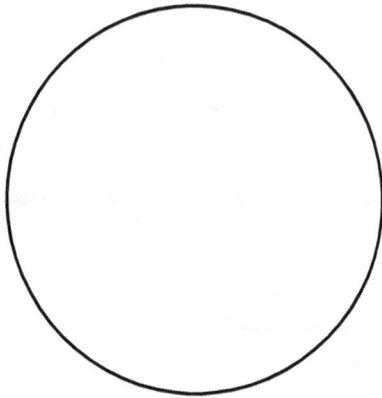

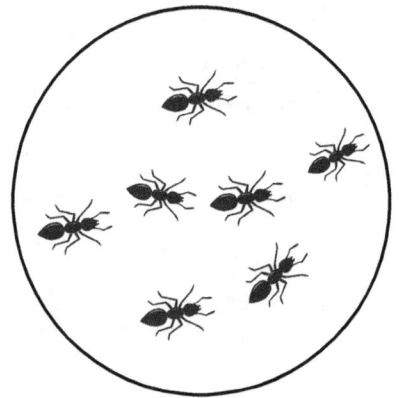

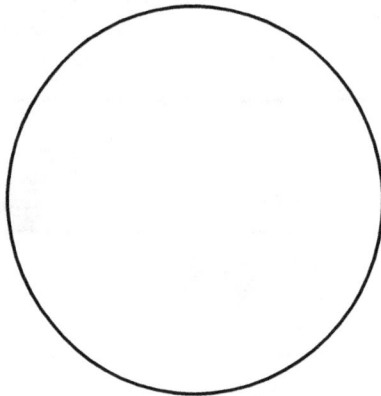

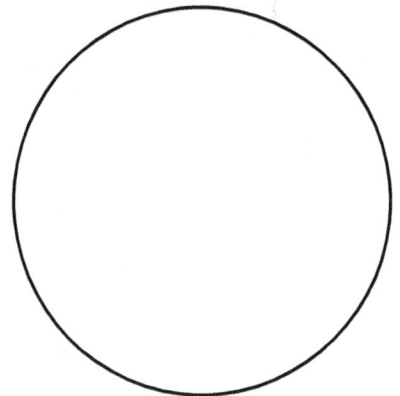

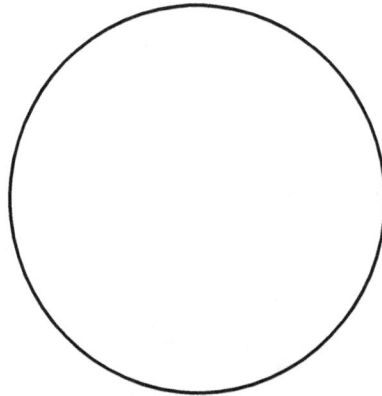

National Park Names

You may be familiar with places designated as a "national park," but this is only one way parks can be named. There are over 400 units (places) in the National Parks Service (NPS) and quite a few ways these places are titled. Certain qualities of parks are reflected in the variety of titles given to them, and these titles offer clues as to what you might find there. Besides the 63 national parks, there are national monuments, national scenic trails, national battlefields, and many more.

The letters of several designations of NPS units are all jumbled up. Can you unscramble the word and figure out the title?

ERRIV

CETERYME

SHSEAREO

ESERVER

ARWAYPK

MRIAEMOL

RELASHOKE

Now arrange the circled letters to solve one last type of NPS unit.

◯ ◯ ◯ ◯ R ◯ ◯ T I ◯ N   A R ◯ ◯

Catch a Fish at Cedar Creek

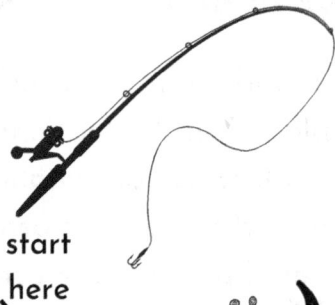

start
here

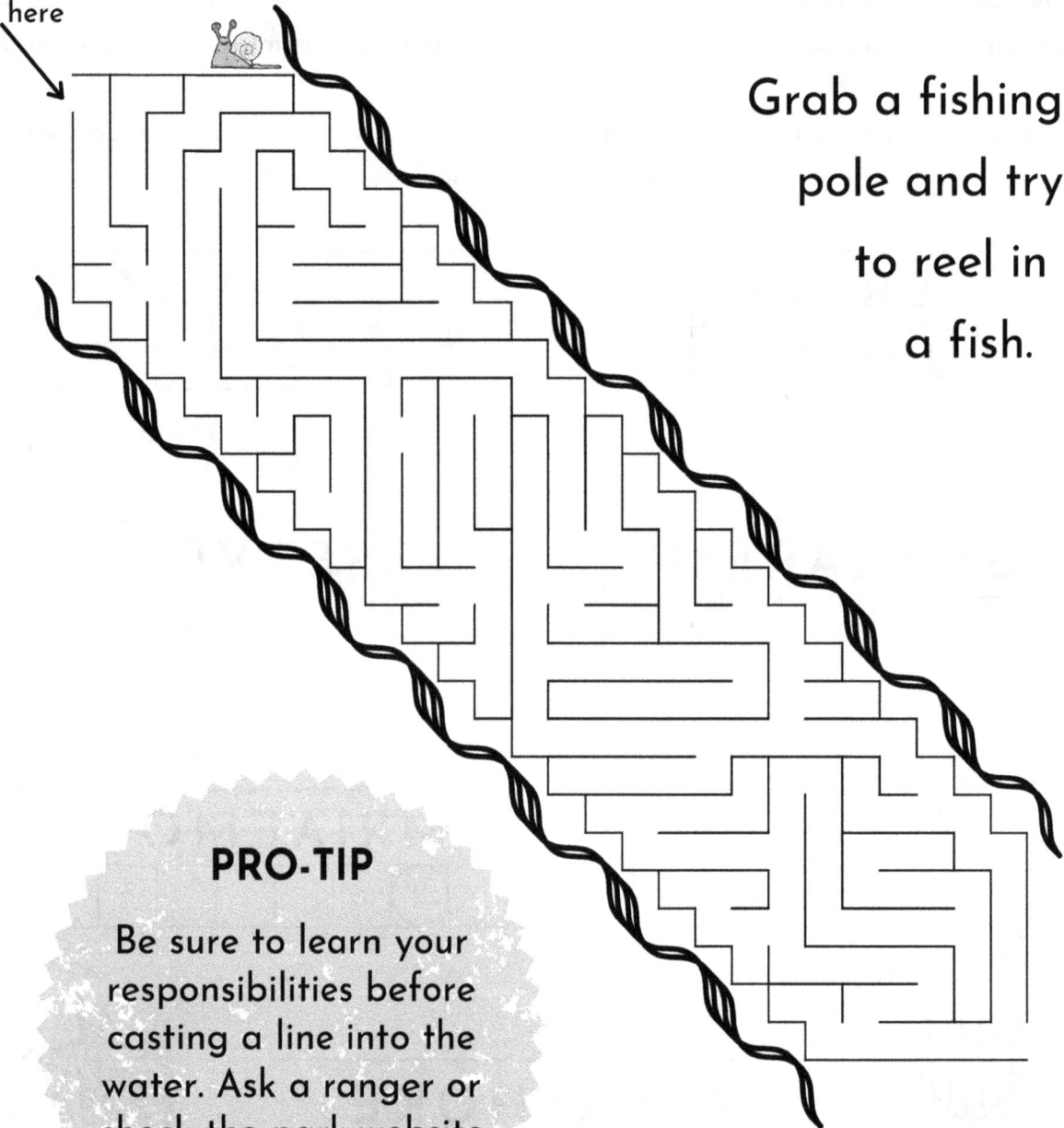

Grab a fishing
pole and try
to reel in
a fish.

PRO-TIP

Be sure to learn your
responsibilities before
casting a line into the
water. Ask a ranger or
check the park website
before you go.

Decoding Using American Sign Language

American Sign Language, also called ASL for short, is a language that many Deaf people or people who are hard of hearing use to communicate. People use ASL to communicate with their hands. Did you know people from all over the country and world travel to national parks? You may hear people speaking other languages. You might also see people using ASL. Use the American Manual Alphabet chart to decode some national parks facts.

This was the first national park to be established:

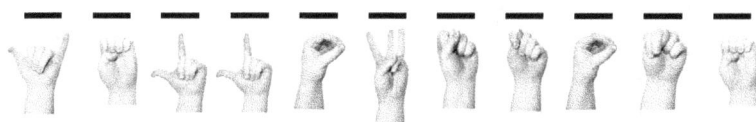

_ _ _ _ _ _ _ _ _ _

This is the biggest national park in the US:

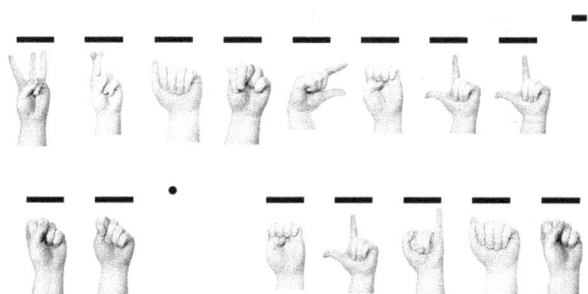

_ _ _ _ _ _ _ _ -

_ _ . _ _ _ _

This is the most visited national park:

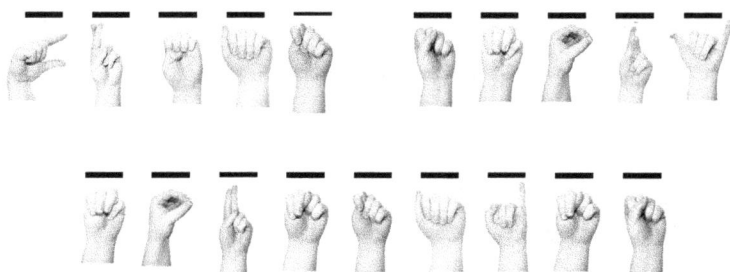

_ _ _ _ _ _ _ _

_ _ _ _ _ _ _

Aa	Bb	Cc	Dd	Ee
Ff	Gg		Hh	Ii
Jj	Kk	Ll	Mm	Nn
Oo	Pp		Qq	Rr
Ss	Tt		Uu	Vv
Ww	Xx		Yy	Zz

Hint: Pay close attention to the position of the thumb!

Try it! Using the chart, try to make the letters of the alphabet with your hand. What is the hardest letter to make? Can you spell out your name? Show a friend or family member and have them watch you spell out the name of the national park you are in.

Go Birdwatching on the Bluff Trail

start here →

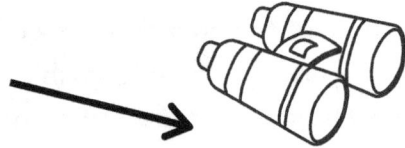

DID YOU KNOW?
Congaree National Park is home to several birds of prey, including eagles, hawks, and owls. Birds of prey are birds that hunt other animals for food.

Butterflies of Congaree

Dozens of species of butterflies and moths live in Congaree National Park. Their wingspan size varies, as do the patterns on their wings. Design your own butterfly below. Make sure the wings are symmetrical, which means both sides match.

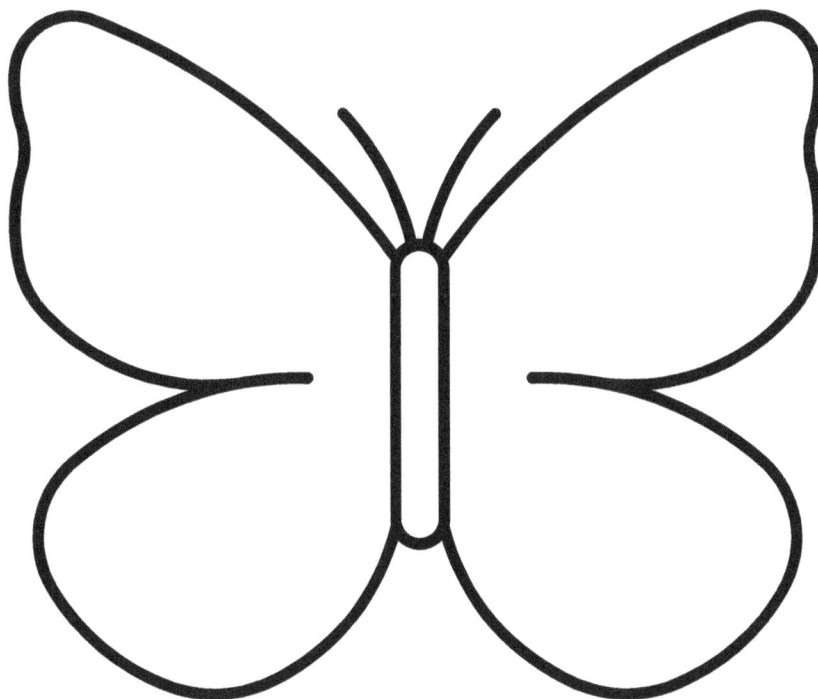

A Hike at Weston Lake

Fill in the blanks on this page without looking at the full story. Once you have each line filled out, use the words you've chosen to complete the story on the next page.

ADJECTIVE --

SOMETHING TO EAT ----------------------------------

SOMETHING TO DRINK --------------------------------

NOUN --

ARTICLE OF CLOTHING -------------------------------

BODY PART ---

VERB --

ANIMAL --

SAME TYPE OF FOOD ---------------------------------

ADJECTIVE ---

SAME ANIMAL ---------------------------------------

VERB THAT ENDS IN "ED" ----------------------------

NUMBER --

A DIFFERENT NUMBER --------------------------------

SOMETHING THAT FLIES ------------------------------

LIGHT SOURCE --------------------------------------

PLURAL NOUN ---------------------------------------

FAMILY MEMBER -------------------------------------

YOUR NICKNAME -------------------------------------

A Hike at Weston Lake

Use the words from the previous page to complete a silly story.

I went for a hike at Weston Lake today. In my favorite _ _ _ _ _ _ _ backpack, I
ADJECTIVE

made sure to pack a map so I wouldn't get lost. I also threw in an extra

_ _ _ _ _ _ _ _ _ _ just in case I got hungry and a bottle of _ _ _ _ _ _ _ _ _ _. I put
SOMETHING TO EAT   SOMETHING TO DRINK

on my _ _ _ _ _ _ _ _ _ spray, and I tied a _ _ _ _ _ _ _ _ _ _ _ _ around my
NOUN   ARTICLE OF CLOTHING

_ _ _ _ _ _ _ _ _ _, in case it gets chilly. I started to _ _ _ _ _ _ down the path. As
BODY PART   VERB

soon as I turned the corner, I came face to face with a(n) _ _ _ _ _ _ _ _. I think
ANIMAL

it was as startled as I was! What should I do? I had to think fast! Should I

give it some of my _ _ _ _ _ _ _ _ _ _ _? No. I had to remember what the
SAME TYPE OF FOOD

_ _ _ _ _ _ _ ranger told me: "If you see one, back away slowly and try not to
ADJECTIVE

scare it." Soon enough, the _ _ _ _ _ _ _ _ _ _   _ _ _ _ _ _ _ _ _ _ away. The coast
SAME ANIMAL   VERB THAT ENDS IN ED

was clear. _ _ _ _ _ _ hours later, I finally reached the lookout. I felt like I could
NUMBER

see for a _ _ _ _ _ _ miles. I took a picture of a _ _ _ _ _ _ _ _ so I could always
A DIFFERENT NUMBER   NOUN

remember this moment. As I was putting my camera away, a _ _ _ _ _ _ _ _ _
SOMETHING THAT FLIES

flew by, reminding me that it was almost nighttime. I turned on my

_ _ _ _ _ _ _ _ _ _ and headed back. I could hear the _ _ _ _ _ _ _ _ _ _ singing their
LIGHT SOURCE   PLURAL INSECT

evening song. Just as I was getting tired, I saw my _ _ _ _ _ _ _ _ _ _ and our tent.
FAMILY MEMBER

"Welcome back _ _ _ _ _ _ _ _! How was your hike?"
NICKNAME

Reducing Your Footprint

Your carbon "footprint" is the amount of carbon dioxide released into the air because of your own energy needs. All people have basic needs like transportation, electricity, food, clothing, and other goods. Governments and private businesses have the biggest impact on the environment, but our individual choices can impact the planet too.

In the box below, make a footprint. You can use your own foot and trace it, step in paint and make a footprint, or draw a footprint freehand.

How does your community try to reduce its carbon footprint? You can use examples from your town, your school, or your family. See page 20 for ideas.

Let's Go Camping at Longleaf

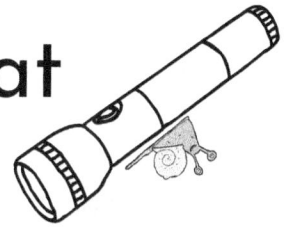

Words may be horizontal, vertical, diagonal, or they might even be backwards!

1. tent
2. camp stove
3. sleeping bag
4. bug spray
5. sunscreen
6. map
7. flashlight
8. pillow
9. lantern
10. ice
11. snacks
12. smores
13. water
14. first aid kit
15. chair
16. cards
17. books
18. games
19. trail
20. hat

```
D P P I L L O W D B T E A C I
E O A D P R E A A M B R C A N
P W C A M P S T O V E I H X G
R A H S G E L E B E E D A P S
E L B U G S P R A Y N G I E A
S I A H G C I C N N M E R C N
C W N L A F I R S K O O B F K
M T A E M I L E L H M R W L J
T A P R E A O R E S L B A A B
S M P A S R R T E N T L U S C
C E A I I R C G P E I U J H A
S S N A C K S S I M O K I L R
I J R S F O I S N J R A Q I D
C Y E T L E V E G U O R V G S
E W T A K C A B B S S O H H M
X J N F I R S T A I D K I T T
U A A E S S E N G E T P V A B
C J L I A R T D N A M A H A S
```

43

All in the Day of a Park Ranger

Park Rangers are hardworking individuals dedicated to protecting our parks, monuments, museums, and more. They take care of the natural and cultural resources for future generations. Rangers also help protect the visitors of the park. Their responsibilities are broad and they work both with the public and behind the scenes.

What have you seen park rangers do? Use your knowledge of the duties of park rangers to fill out a typical daily schedule, listing one activity for each hour. Feel free to make up your own, but some examples of activities are provided on the right. Read carefully! Not all the example activities are befitting a ranger.

6 am	Lead a sunrise hike
7 am	
8 am	
9 am	
10 am	
11 am	
12 pm	Enjoy a lunch break outside
1 pm	
2 pm	
3 pm	
4 pm	Teach visitors about the ecology of the river
5 pm	
6 pm	
7 pm	
8 pm	
9 pm	

- feed the migratory birds
- build trails for visitors to enjoy
- throw rocks off the side of the boardwalk
- rescue lost hikers
- study animal behavior
- record air quality data
- answer questions at the visitor center
- pick wildflowers
- pick up litter
- share marshmallows with squirrels
- repair handrails
- lead a class on a field trip
- catch frogs or toads and make them race
- lead people on educational hikes
- write articles for the park website
- protect the river from pollution
- remove non-native plants from the park
- study how climate change is affecting the park
- give a talk about snakes
- lead a program for campers on champion trees.

If you were a park ranger, which of the above tasks would you enjoy most?

_____

Draw Yourself as a Park Ranger

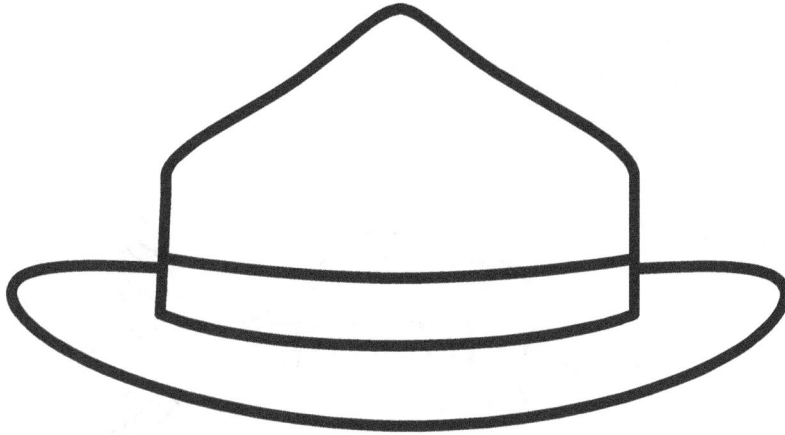

RANGER

Fish of The Congaree River

1.
HDAS

Unscramble the common names of these fish that live in the park.

2.
RCHPE

3.
HISNER

4.
NFUISHS

Word Bank

5.
SABS

1. _____
2. _____
3. _____
4. _____
5. _____

shad
sunfish
perch
minnow
sculpin
bass
shiner
catfish

Amphibians

Two species of toad and twenty-three species of frogs live in Congaree National Park. Even more types of salamanders live there too. Frogs and toads both spend the beginning of their lives the same way - as tadpoles. Tadpoles hatch from eggs, usually in springs or pools of water.

Both frogs and toads are amphibians. Salamanders are amphibians too. Color the amphibians below.

Sound Exploration

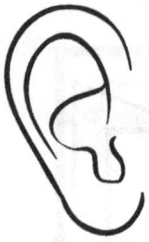

Spend a minute or two listening to all of the sounds around you.
Draw your favorite sound.

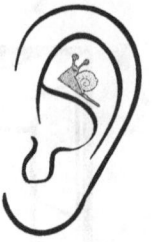

How did this sound make you feel?

_____

_____

What did you think when you heard this sound?

_____

_____

Draw a Squirrel

Complete the picture below by drawing the other half of the squirrel. Finish the image by coloring it in.

Several species of squirrels call Congaree home. Have you seen any of them in the park?

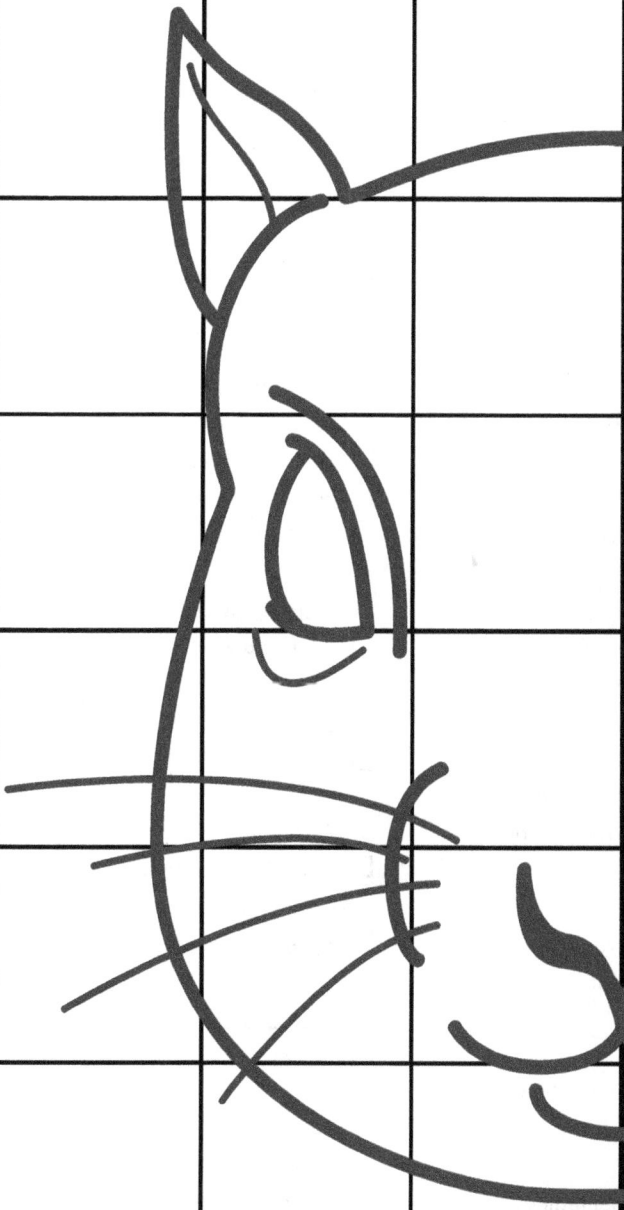

63 National Parks

How many other national parks have you been to? Which one do you want to visit next? Note that if some of these parks fall on the border of more than one state, you may check it off more than once!

Alaska
- [ ] Denali National Park
- [ ] Gates of the Arctic National Park
- [ ] Glacier Bay National Park
- [ ] Katmai National Park
- [ ] Kenai Fjords National Park
- [ ] Kobuk Valley National Park
- [ ] Lake Clark National Park
- [ ] Wrangell-St. Elias National Park

American Samoa
- [ ] National Park of American Samoa

Arizona
- [ ] Grand Canyon National Park
- [ ] Petrified Forest National Park
- [ ] Saguaro National Park

Arkansas
- [ ] Hot Springs National Park

California
- [ ] Channel Islands National Park
- [ ] Death Valley National Park
- [ ] Joshua Tree National Park
- [ ] Kings Canyon National Park
- [ ] Lassen Volcanic National Park
- [ ] Pinnacles National Park
- [ ] Redwood National Park
- [ ] Sequoia National Park
- [ ] Yosemite National Park

Colorado
- [ ] Black Canyon of the Gunnison National Park
- [ ] Great Sand Dunes National Park
- [ ] Mesa Verde National Park
- [ ] Rocky Mountain National Park

Florida
- [ ] Biscayne National Park
- [ ] Dry Tortugas National Park
- [ ] Everglades National Park

Hawaii
- [ ] Haleakalā National Park
- [ ] Hawai'i Volcanoes National Park

Idaho
- [ ] Yellowstone National Park

Kentucky
- [ ] Mammoth Cave National Park

Indiana
- [ ] Indiana Dunes National Park

Maine
- [ ] Acadia National Park

Michigan
- [ ] Isle Royale National Park

Minnesota
- [ ] Voyageurs National Park

Missouri
- [ ] Gateway Arch National Park

Montana
- [ ] Glacier National Park
- [ ] Yellowstone National Park

Nevada
- [ ] Death Valley National Park
- [ ] Great Basin National Park

New Mexico
- [ ] Carlsbad Caverns National Park
- [ ] White Sands National Park

North Dakota
- [ ] Theodore Roosevelt National Park

North Carolina
- [ ] Great Smoky Mountains National Park

Ohio
- [ ] Cuyahoga Valley National Park

Oregon
- [ ] Crater Lake National Park

South Carolina
- [ ] Congaree National Park

South Dakota
- [ ] Badlands National Park
- [ ] Wind Cave National Park

Tennessee
- [ ] Great Smoky Mountains National Park

Texas
- [ ] Big Bend National Park
- [ ] Guadalupe Mountains National Park

Utah
- [ ] Arches National Park
- [ ] Bryce Canyon National Park
- [ ] Canyonlands National Park
- [ ] Capitol Reef National Park
- [ ] Zion National Park

Virgin Islands
- [ ] Virgin Islands National Park

Virginia
- [ ] Shenandoah National Park

Washington
- [ ] Mount Rainier National Park
- [ ] North Cascades National Park
- [ ] Olympic National Park

West Virginia
- [ ] New River Gorge National Park

Wyoming
- [ ] Grand Teton National Park
- [ ] Yellowstone National Park

Other National Parks Crossword

Besides Congaree National Park, there are 62 other diverse and beautiful national parks across the United States. Try your hand at this crossword. If you need help, look at the previous page for some hints.

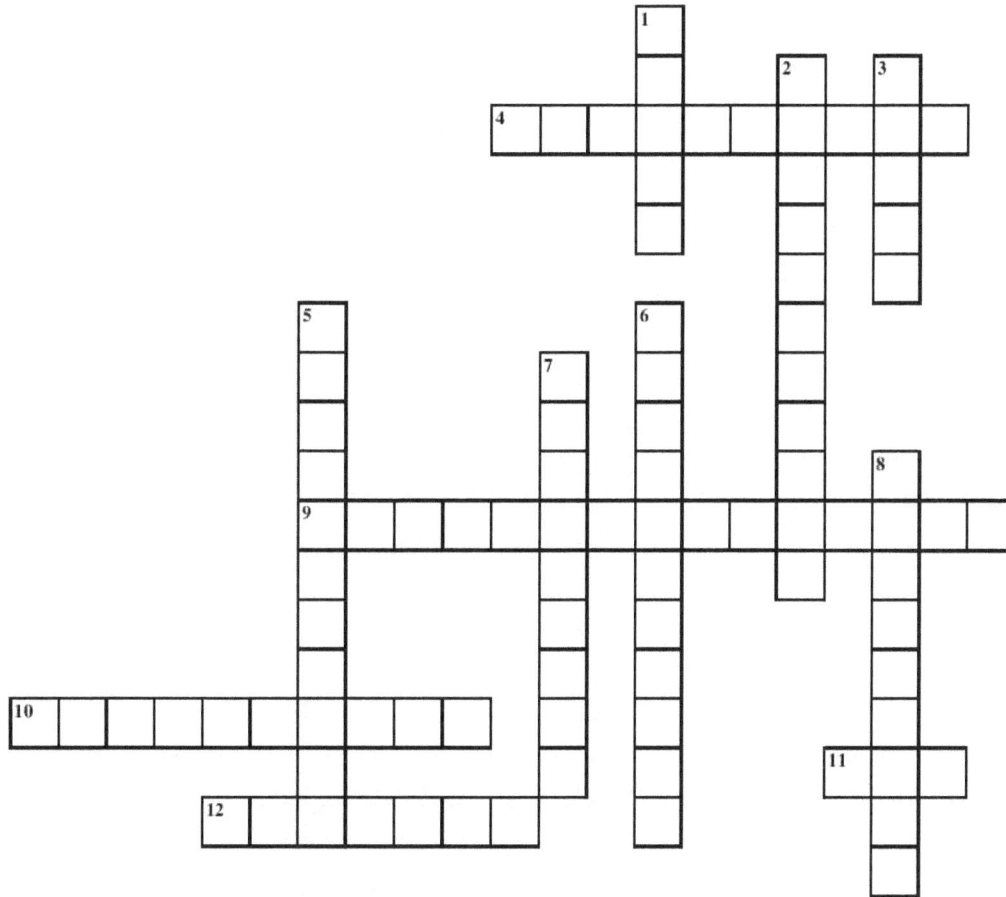

Down

1. State where Acadia National Park is located
2. This national park has the Spanish word for turtle in it
3. Number of national parks in Alaska
5. This national park has some of the hottest temperatures in the world
6. This national park is the only one in Idaho
7. This toothsome creature can famously be found in Everglades National Park
8. Only president with a national park named for them

Across

4. This state has the most national parks
9. This park has some of the newest land in the US, caused by volcanic eruptions
10. This park has the deepest lake in the United States
11. This color shows up in the name of a national park in California
12. This national park deserves a gold medal

Which National Park Will You Go To Next?
Word Search

1. Zion
2. Big Bend
3. Glacier
4. Olympic
5. Sequoia
6. Bryce
7. Mesa Verde
8. Biscayne
9. Wind Cave
10. Great Basin
11. Katmai
12. Yellowstone
13. Voyageurs
14. Arches
15. Badlands
16. Denali
17. Glacier Bay
18. Hot Springs

```
F M M E S A V E R D E B N E Y
E A B I G B E N D E S A S E M
Y L I C A L O Y N E E D L T G
D M G A S S A U C N R L U E R
C E L I I T S C R E O A A K E
S N A W Y E E O I W T N A C A
G I C H A A Q C S E M D N S T
N O I Z P R U T I M R S N E B
I W E L M P O N B W E B K H A
R J R F D N I F L I H B U C S
P A B E E S A N E S O P W R I
S J A E N Y A C S I B A U A N
T C Y I A D O H H Y M E A L R
O T A T L M L E S E G R W R J
H S T O I K A T M A I R O P B
I C H U R C O L Y M P I C O U
O Y G T S D E O S B R Y C E T
W I N D C A V E I N R O H E M
```

Field Notes

Spend some time reflecting on your trip to Congaree National Park. Your field notes will help you remember the things you experienced. Use the space below to write about your day.

While I was at Congaree National Park...

I saw:

_____

_____

_____

_____

I heard:

_____

_____

_____

I felt:

_____

_____

Draw a picture of your favorite thing in the park.

_____

I wondered:

_____

_____

_____

_____

_____

ANSWER KEY

Go Canoeing on the Congaree River Blue Trail

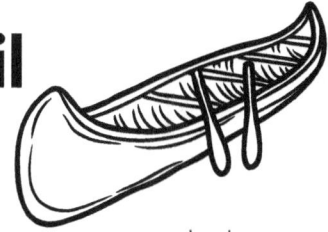

start here →

DID YOU KNOW?

The Congaree River Blue Trail is a 50-mile designated recreational paddling trail, extending from the state capital of Columbia, downstream to Congaree National Park.

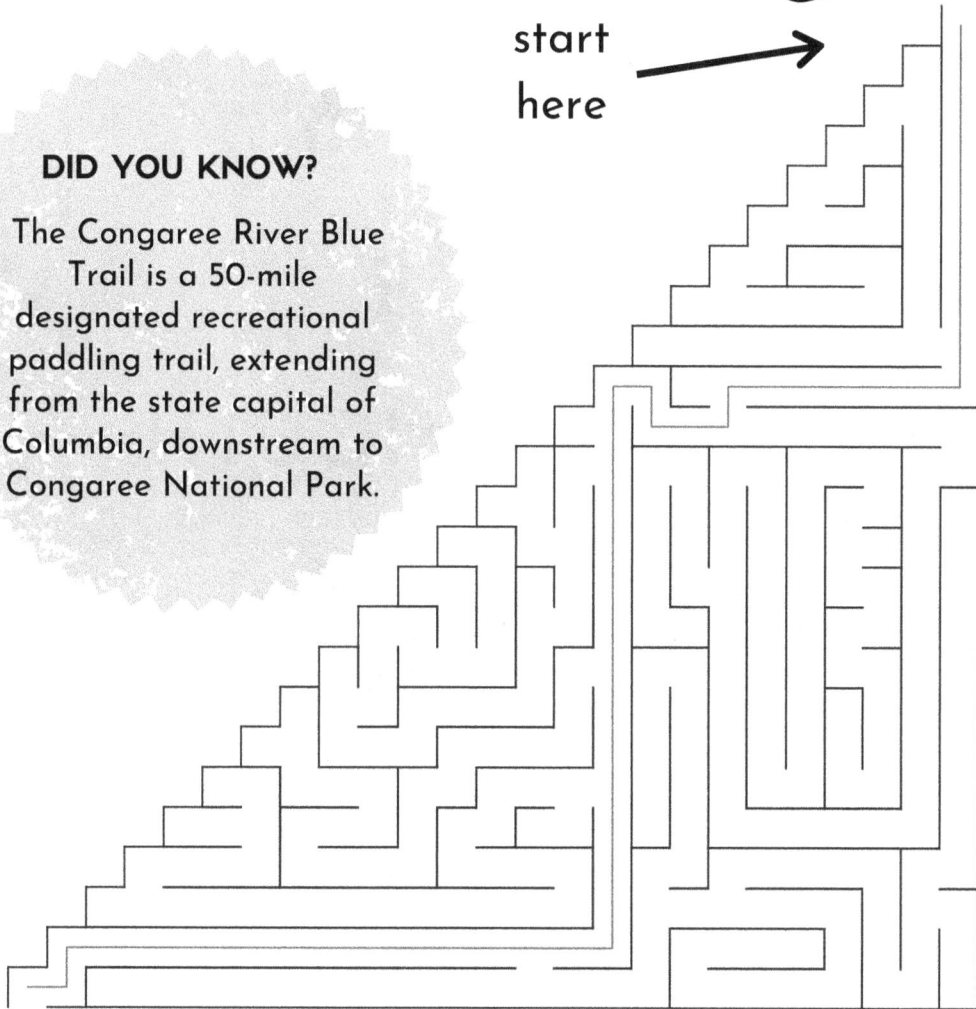

Answers: Who lives here?

Below are 8 plants and animals that live in the park.
Use the word bank to fill in the clues below.

WORD BANK: BEAVER, OSPREY, ALLIGATOR, COYOTE, BUCKEYE,
COTTONMOUTH, BOBCAT, VELVET ANT

BU C KEYE

COY O TE

COTTO N MOUTH

ALLI G ATOR

BOBC A T

OSPR E Y

VELVE T ■ ANT

B E AVER

Find the Match!
Common Names and Latin Names

Match the common name to the scientific name for each animal. The first one is done for you. Use clues on the page before and after this one to complete the matches.

Gray Fox   Haliaeetus leucocephalus

Loblolly Pine   Lontra canadensis

Cypress   Butorides virescens

River Otter   Sylvilagus palustris

Great Horned Owl   Pinus taeda

Bald Eagle   Agkistrodon contortrix

Green Heron   Bubo virginianus

Marsh Rabbit   Urocyon cinereoargenteus

Copperhead   Taxodium distichum

Bald Eagle

Haliaeetus leucocephalus

Jumbles Answers

1. KAYAKING
2. HIKING
3. BIRDING
4. CAMPING
5. PICNICKING
6. SIGHTSEEING
7. STAR GAZING

Map Symbol Sudoku Anwers

🚶	🏠	🔭	⛺
⛺	🔭	🏠	🚶
🏠	🚶	⛺	🔭
🔭	⛺	🚶	🏠

National Park Emblem Answers

1. This represents all plants: **Sequoia Tree**

2. This represents all animals: **Bison**

3. This represents the landscapes: **Mountains**

4. This represents the waters protected by the park service: **Water**

5. This represents the historical and archeological values: **Arrowhead**

Answers: The Ten Essentials

Careful preparation and knowledge are key to a successful adventure into Congaree's backcountry.

The ten essentials are a list of things that are important to have when you go for longer hikes. If you go on a hike to the <u>backcountry</u>, it is especially important that you have everything you need in case of an emergency. If you get lost or something unforeseen happens, it is good to be prepared to survive until help finds you.

The ten essentials list was developed in the 1930s by an outdoors group called the Mountaineers. Over time and technological advancements, this list has evolved. Can you identify all the things on the current list? Circle each of the "essentials" and cross out everything that doesn't make the cut.

(fire: matches, lighter, tinder, and/or stove)	~~a pint of milk~~	~~extra money~~	(headlamp, plus extra batteries)	(extra clothes)
(extra water)	~~a dog~~	~~Polaroid camera~~	~~bug net~~	~~lightweight game like a deck of cards~~
(extra food)	~~a roll of duct tape~~	(shelter)	(sun protection, such as sunglasses, sun-protective clothes and sunscreen)	(knife, plus a gear repair kit)
~~a mirror~~	(navigation: map, compass, altimeter, GPS device, or satellite messenger)	(first aid kit)	~~extra flip-flops~~	~~entertainment like video games or books~~

Backcountry - a remote undeveloped rural area.

Congaree Word Search

Words may be horizontal, vertical, diagonal,
or they might even be backwards!

1. mosquitos
2. boardwalk
3. cypresses
4. turtles
5. woodpeckers
6. snakes
7. swamp
8. south
9. carolina
10. floodplain
11. bottomland
12. oxbow
13. fireflies
14. knees
15. eastover
16. southeast
17. sierra club

```
O  X  B  O  W  T  H  W  E  S  T  L  O  W  C
A  B  O  A  R  D  W  A  L  K  E  L  A  N  A
N  G  K  S  O  T  I  U  Q  S  O  M  A  F  N
I  M  P  N  Y  T  H  T  W  O  R  G  D  L  O
L  I  A  D  E  A  L  L  O  E  I  S  I  O  E
O  O  N  D  D  E  A  A  D  C  T  W  K  O  I
R  E  S  E  E  H  S  O  U  T  H  A  I  D  N
A  L  B  A  N  U  I  E  G  E  N  M  N  P  G
C  Y  P  R  E  S  S  E  S  B  C  P  G  L  E
P  C  T  S  A  E  H  T  U  O  S  I  O  A  A
T  U  R  T  L  E  S  L  O  I  K  E  T  I  N
S  R  N  I  K  O  C  I  O  V  O  K  I  N  E
N  I  O  F  E  A  S  T  O  V  E  R  L  G  W
A  C  G  F  R  O  V  E  P  O  O  R  V  E  H
K  I  L  R  K  D  N  A  L  M  O  T  T  O  B
E  T  E  I  A  E  E  G  E  Z  E  P  R  N  L
S  I  W  O  O  D  P  E  C  K  E  R  S  I  E
S  E  I  L  F  E  R  I  F  Y  M  A  L  A  Z
```

60

Wildlife Wisdom

The national park is home to many different kinds of animals. Seeing wildlife can be an exciting part of visiting the national park but it is important to remember that these animals are wild. They need plenty of space and a healthy habitat where they can find their own food. Part of this is not allowing animals to eat any human food. This is their home and we are the visitors. We need to be respectful of the wildlife in the park.

Directions: Circle the highlighted words that best complete the following sentences.

If an animal changes its behavior because of your presence, you are:
A) too close
B) funny looking
C) dehydrated and should drink more water

The best thing we can do to help wild animals survive is:
A) make them pets
B) protect their habitat
C) knit them winter sweaters

In a national park, it is okay to share your food with wild animals:
A) never
B) always
C) sometimes

When you're hiking in an area where there are bears, you should warn bears that you are entering their space by:
A) hiking quietly
B) making noise
C) wearing bright colors

At night, park rangers care for the animals by:
A) putting them back into their cages
B) tucking them into bed
C) leaving them alone

If you see an abandoned bird's nest, it is best to:
A) pet the baby birds
B) leave it alone
C) crunch the empty eggshells

Bears look under logs in hopes of finding:
A) granola bars
B) insects
C) peanuts to eat

The place where an animal lives is called its:
A) condo
B) habitat
C) crib

Solution:
Hike the Boardwalk
Loop Trail

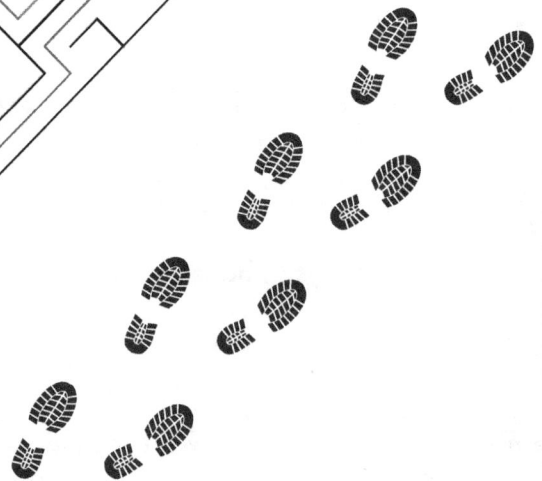

DID YOU KNOW?
About 80% of the park lies within the floodplains of the Congaree River, these boardwalks allow visitors to explore!

Congaree Waterways
Word Search

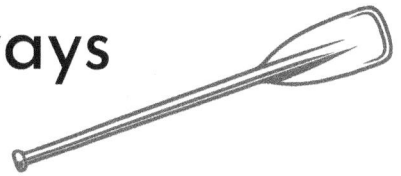

Congaree National Park is a floodplain forest. Waters from the Congaree and Wateree Rivers sweep through the floodplain, carrying nutrients and sediments that nourish and rejuvenate this ecosystem.

1. canoe
2. kayak
3. paddle
4. alligator
5. Cedar Creek
6. old-growth
7. safety
8. hazard
9. log jam
10. caution
11. aquatic
12. habitat
13. turtle
14. snag
15. explore
16. water

H A B I T A T R E S K L O W K
H T A S K I L E R O L P X E J
T E P R C A N O E C L B A P B
S M P A G P T U R T L E U H C
C E C E D A R C R E E K J A L
A O L D G C O A E C T E A Z I
R E S I E H E K L N K A Y A K
P L L A M U I E D W N E K R G
R L H S G M L O D E I D Y D M
A C C I T A U Q A I P H O E A
L O G J A M I N P O K T N S N
S R N I K O S I S M O W I R P
W I O S N I A L P D O O L F W
A C G O L O F E S O O R V E H
T I C C A U T I O N A G A N S
E T T F A E E G L Z E D Q N L
R Y D R O E Y E C T R L C E E
C J D O S N E D N Y M O L A M

Answers: Leave No Trace Quiz

1. How can you plan ahead and prepare to ensure you have the best experience you can in the National Park?
    A. Make sure you stop by the ranger station for a map and to ask about current conditions.
2. What is an example of traveling on a durable surface?
    A. Walking only on the designated path.
3. Why should you dispose of waste properly?
    C. So that other peoples' experiences of the park are not impacted by you leaving your waste behind.
4. How can you best follow the concept "leave what you find?"
    B. Take pictures but leave any physical items where they are.
5. What is not a good example of minimizing campfire impacts?
    C. Building a new campfire ring in a location that has a better view.
6. What is a poor example of respecting wildlife?
    A. Building squirrel houses out of rocks from the river so the squirrels have a place to live.
7. How can you show consideration of other visitors?
    B. Wear headphones on the trail if you choose to listen to music.

Answers: National Park Names

ERRIV
R I V E R

CETERYME
C E M E T E R Y

SHSEAREO
S E A S H O R E

ESERVER
R E S E R V E

ARWAYPK
P A R K W A Y

MRIAEMOL
M E M O R I A L

RELASHOKE
L A K E S H O R E

Now arrange the circled letters to solve one last type of NPS unit.

R E C R E A T I O N   A R E A

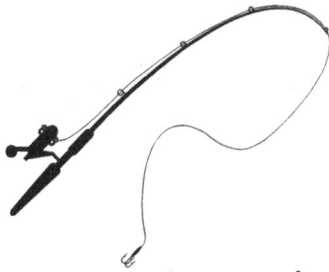

Solution: Catch a Fish at Cedar Creek

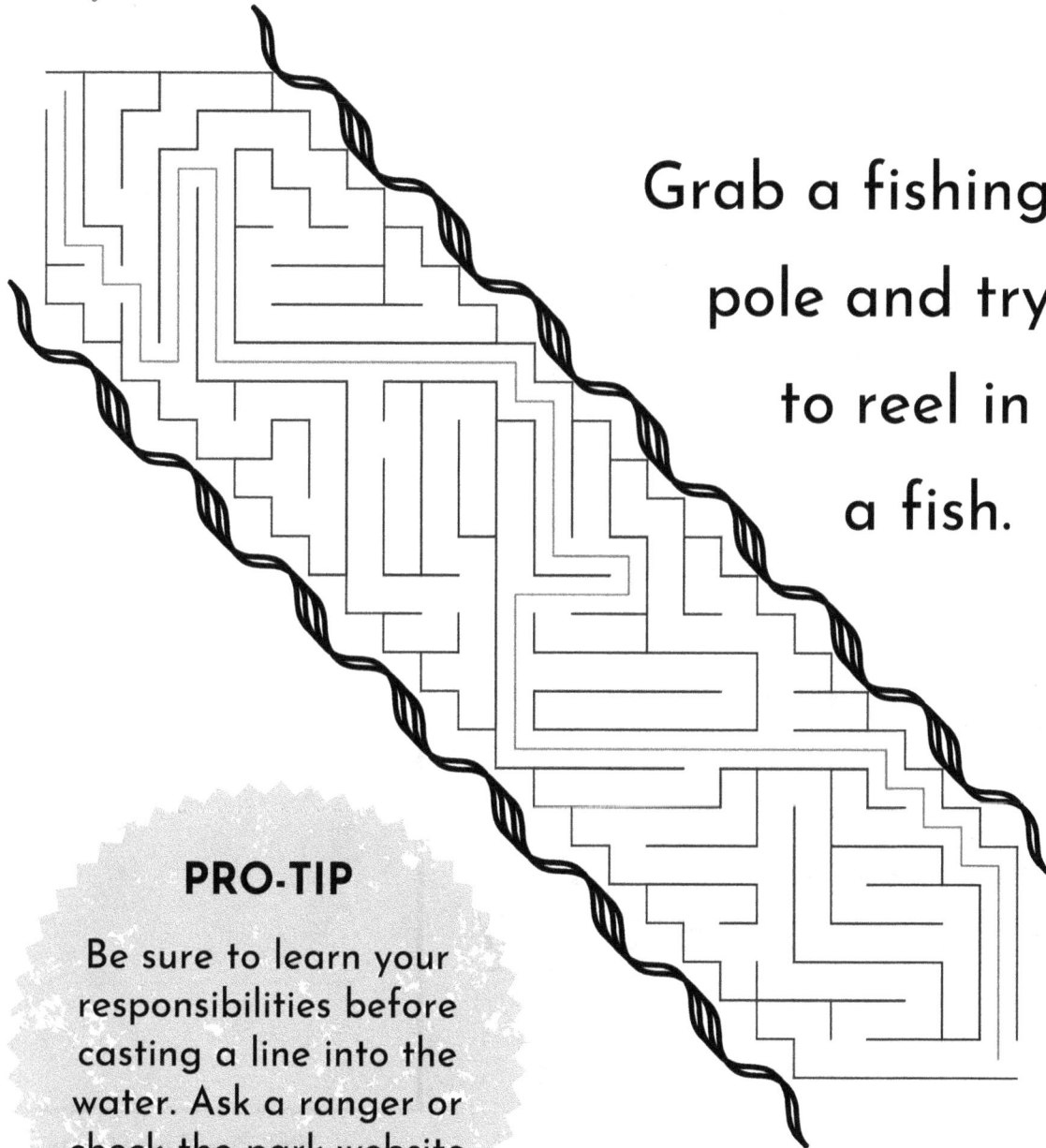

Grab a fishing pole and try to reel in a fish.

PRO-TIP

Be sure to learn your responsibilities before casting a line into the water. Ask a ranger or check the park website before you go.

Decoding Using American Sign Language

American Sign Language, also called ASL for short, is a language that many Deaf people or people who are hard of hearing use to communicate. People use ASL to communicate with their hands. Did you know people from all over the country and world travel to national parks? You may hear people speaking other languages. You might also see people using ASL. Use the American Manual Alphabet chart to decode some national parks facts.

This was the first national park to be established:

Y E L L O W S T O N E

This is the biggest national park in the US:

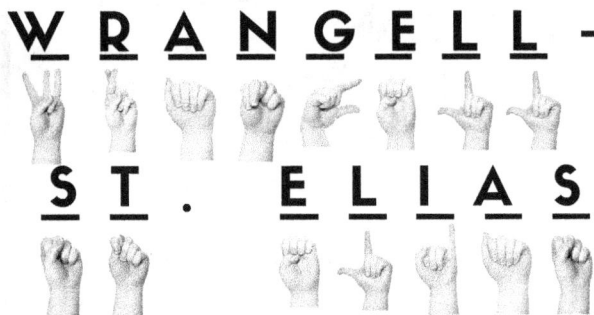

W R A N G E L L -

S T . E L I A S

This is the most visited national park:

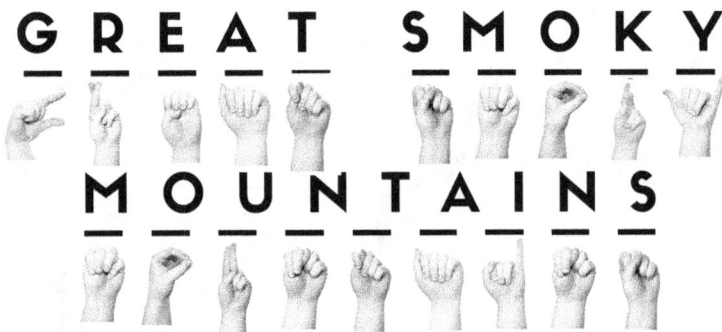

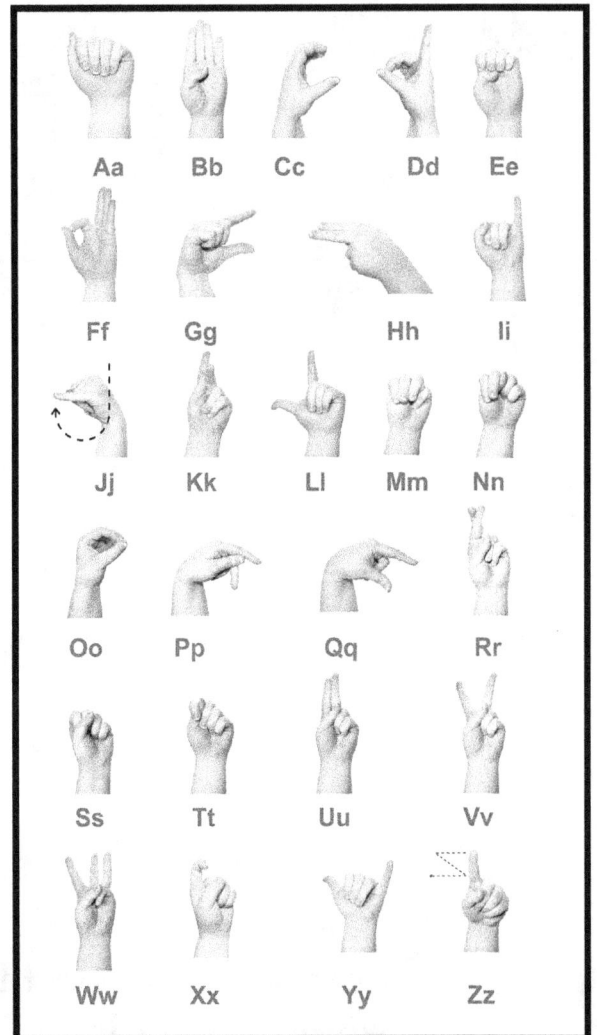

G R E A T   S M O K Y

M O U N T A I N S

Aa	Bb	Cc	Dd	Ee
Ff	Gg		Hh	Ii
Jj	Kk	Ll	Mm	Nn
Oo	Pp		Qq	Rr
Ss	Tt		Uu	Vv
Ww	Xx		Yy	Zz

Hint: Pay close attention to the position of the thumb!

Try it! Using the chart, try to make the letters of the alphabet with your hand. What is the hardest letter to make? Can you spell out your name? Show a friend or family member and have them watch you spell out the name of the national park you are in.

Go Birdwatching at Bluff Trail

start here

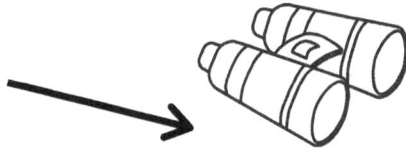

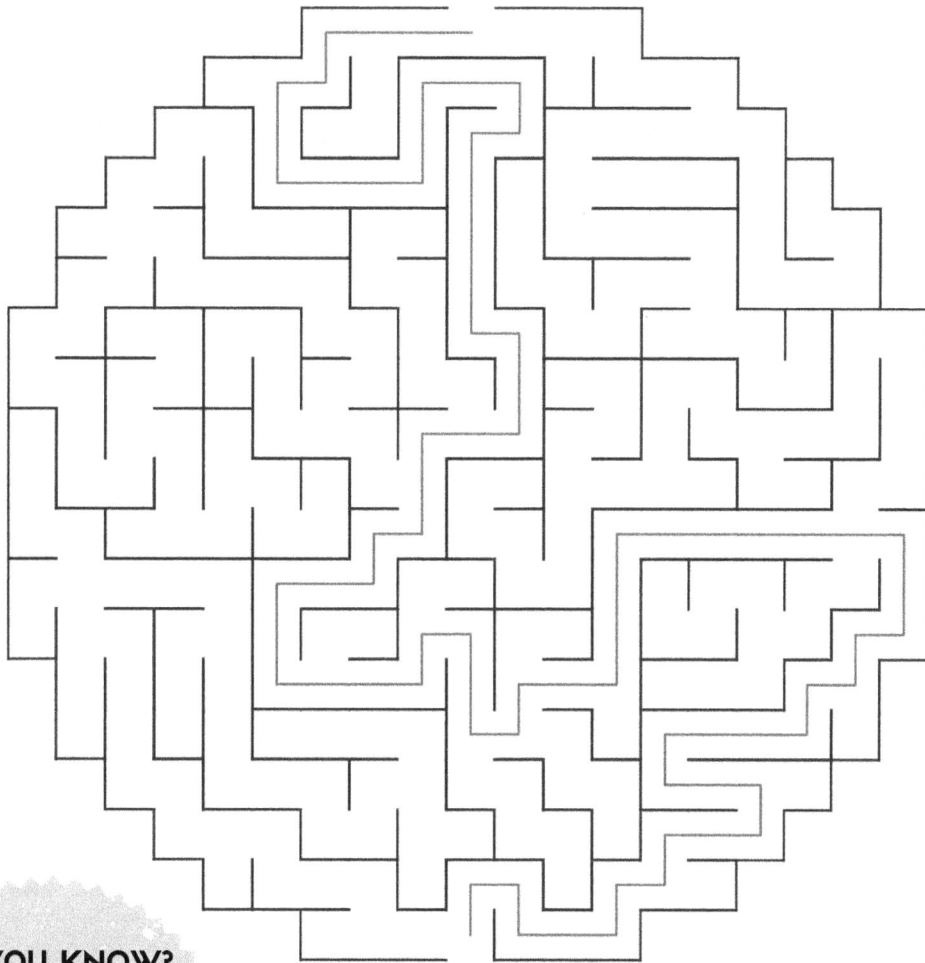

DID YOU KNOW?
Congaree NP is home to several birds of prey, including eagles, hawks, and owls. Birds of prey are birds that hunt other animals for food.

Let's Go Camping
at Longleaf

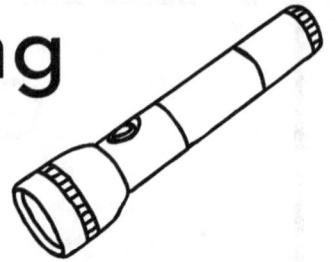

1. tent
2. camp stove
3. sleeping bag
4. bug spray
5. sunscreen
6. map
7. flashlight
8. pillow
9. lantern
10. ice
11. snacks
12. smores
13. water
14. first aid kit
15. chair
16. cards
17. books
18. games
19. trail
20. hat

```
D P P I L L O W D B T E A C I
E O A D P R E A A M B R C A N
P W C A M P S T O V E I H X G
R A H S G E L E B E E D A P S
E L B U G S P R A Y N G I E A
S I A H G C I C N N M E R C N
C W N L A F I R S K O O B F K
M T A E M I L E L H M R W L J
T A P R E A O R E S L B A A B
S M P A S R R T E N T L U S C
C E A I I R C G P E I U J H A
S S N A C K S S I M O K I L R
I J R S F O I S N J R A Q I D
C Y E T L E V E G U O R V G S
E W T A K C A B B S S O H H M
X J N F I R S T A I D K I T T
U A A E S S E N G E T P V A B
C J L I A R T D N A M A H A S
```

68

All in the Day of a Park Ranger

There are many right answers for this activity, but not all of the provided examples are good activities for a park ranger. In fact, a park ranger's job may include stopping visitors from doing some of these things.

The list below are activities that rangers do not do:

feed the migratory birds

throw rocks off the side of the boardwalk

pick wildflowers

share marshmallows with squirrels

catch frogs or toads and make them race

Fish of The Congaree River

1. SHAD
2. PERCH
3. SHINER
4. SUNFISH
5. BASS

Answers: Other National Parks Crossword

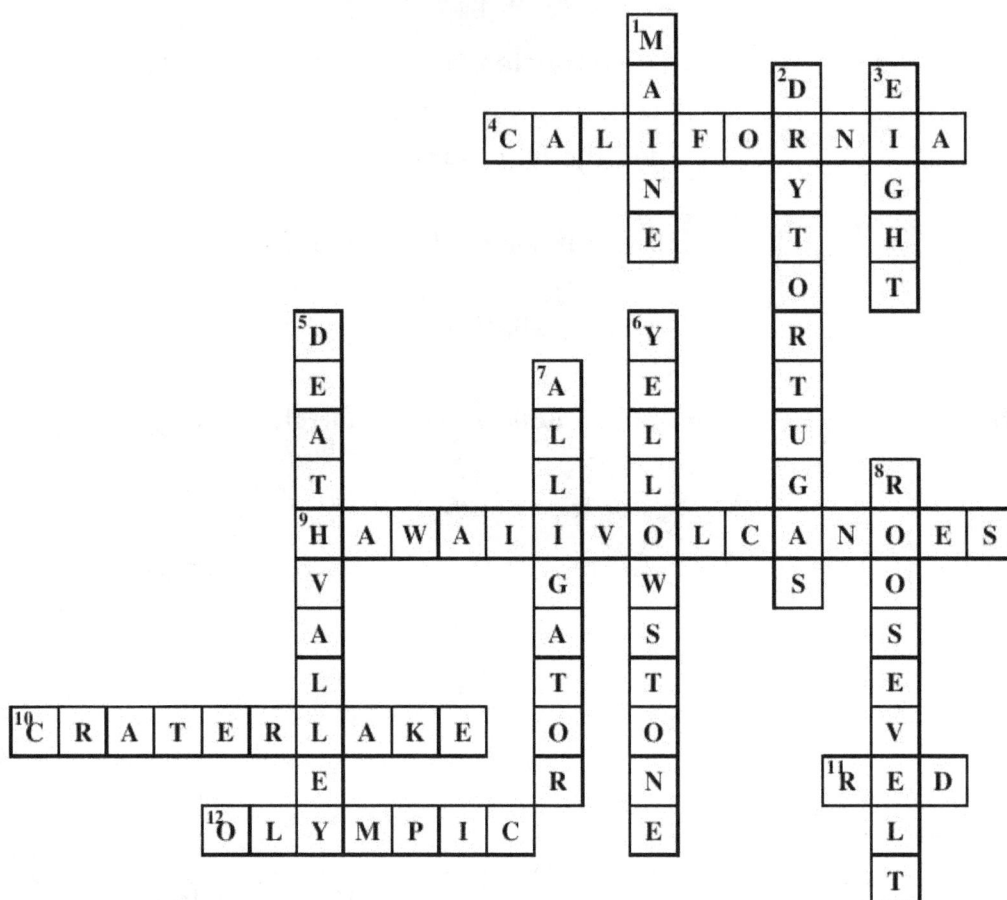

The crossword answer grid:

- 1 Down: MAINE
- 4 Across: CALIFORNIA
- 2 Down: DRYTORTUGAS
- 3 Down: EIGHT
- 5 Down: DEATHVALLEY
- 6 Down: YELLOWSTONE
- 7 Down: ALLIGATOR
- 8 Down: ROOSEVELT
- 9 Across: HAWAIIVOLCANOES
- 10 Across: CRATERLAKE
- 11 Across: RED
- 12 Across: OLYMPIC

Down

1. State where Acadia National Park is located
2. This National Park has the Spanish word for turtle in it
3. Number of National Parks in Alaska
5. This National Park has some of the hottest temperatures in the world
6. This National Park is the only one in Idaho
7. This toothsome creature can famously be found in Everglades National Park
8. Only president with a national park named for them

Across

4. This state has the most National Parks
9. This park has some of the newest land in the US, caused by a volcanic eruption
10. This park has the deepest lake in the United States
11. This color shows up in the name of a National Park in California
12. This National Park deserves a gold medal

Answers: Which National Park Will You Go To Next?

1. Zion
2. Big Bend
3. Glacier
4. Olympic
5. Sequoia
6. Bryce
7. Mesa Verde
8. Biscayne
9. Wind Cave
10. Great Basin
11. Katmai
12. Yellowstone
13. Voyageurs
14. Arches
15. Badlands
16. Denali
17. Glacier Bay
18. Hot Springs

```
F M M E S A V E R D E B N E Y
E A B I G B E N D E S A S E M
Y L I C A L O Y N E E D L T G
D M G A S S A U C N R L U E R
C E L I I T S C R E O A A K E
S N A W Y E E O I W T N A C A
G I C H A A Q C S E M D N S T
N O I Z P R U T I M R S N E B
I W E L M P O N B W E B K H A
R J R F D N I F L I H B U C S
P A B E E S A N E S O P W R I
S J A E N Y A C S I B A U A N
T C Y I A D O H H Y M E A L R
O T A T L M L E S E G R W R J
H S T O I K A T M A I R O P B
I C H U R C O L Y M P I C O U
O Y G T S D E O S B R Y C E T
W I N D C A V E I N R O H E M
```

LITTLE BISON

Press

Little Bison Press is an independent children's book publisher based in the Pacific Northwest. We promote exploration, conservation, and adventure through our books. Established in 2021, our passion for outside spaces and travel inspired the creation of Little Bison Press.

We seek to publish books that support children in learning about and caring for the natural places in our world.

To learn more, visit:
www.littlebisonpress.com

Want more free games and activities? Visit our website!